LEARN CHESS
fast

bright sky press

Albany, Texas • New York, New York

**Library of Congress
Cataloging-in-Publication Data**

Keene, Raymond D.
Learn chess fast : the fun way to start smart and
master the game / by Raymond Keene and
Nancy K. Stewart ; [illustrations by Roxie Munro].
p. cm.

Summary: Provides instruction in the basics of playing
chess, using illustrated explanations, diagrams, stories,
and quotations, as well as examples of elementary
games and strategies.
ISBN 0-9704729-4-3 (pbk.) – ISBN 0-9704729-5-1
(boxed kit)
1. Chess—Juvenile literature. [1. Chess.] I. Stewart,
Nancy K., 1956- II. Munro, Roxie, ill. III. Title.

GV1446 .K427 2001
794.1—dc21   2001037802

Book and cover design by Caroline Brock

Illustrations by Roxie Munro

Distributed by: Sterling Publishing Co., Inc.

Printed in China

LEARN CHESS

**THE FUN WAY
TO START SMART
& MASTER THE GAME**

fast

Raymond Keene, OBE & Nancy K. Stewart
Illustrations by Roxie Munro

bright sky press
Albany, Texas • New York, New York

This book is dedicated to
Alexander, Helen, Merlin and Sarah,
without whom
it would not have been written!

TABLE OF CONTENTS

FIRST THINGS FIRST...

WHY IS CHESS SO COOL?

Chess is aggressive — you fight.

Chess is competitive — you win.

Chess is sociable — you play at home, at school, in clubs, and, increasingly, by e-mail.

Chess makes you think.

Chess is creative — no two games are ever alike. Games that focus on strategy make you spend more time planning than actually playing. In tactical games, you react to your opponent instead of acting independently.

CHESS IS A NEAR PERFECT MIXTURE OF STRATEGY AND TACTICS.

You choose the kind of game you want to play: reckless or careful, cunning or straightforward. This is the strategic part. The tactics come in as you constantly revise your plan during the game.

Because chess is about winning, it is also about losing. You learn more about the game by losing to an experienced player than by always beating beginners. Winning is fun, but losing and coming back

> "'I declare it's marked out just like a large chessboard!' Alice said at last. 'There ought to be some men moving about somewhere — and so there are!'"
>
> — *Alice Through the Looking Glass* by Lewis Carroll

Bishop

Rook

Queen

Pawn

King

Knight

for more requires real toughness and self-control.

Chess players don't get angry — they get even. They keep trying.

WHO PLAYS CHESS?

Two people play chess, one with sixteen white pieces, the other with sixteen black ones. The game starts with these pieces lined up at either end of a checkered board. The players take turns moving their own chessmen one at a time.

WHO WINS?

The winner is the player who blocks off all the enemy king's escape routes so that the king would be captured in the next move. This is called checkmate.

IN A CHESS GAME THE LOSING KING IS NEVER ACTUALLY LIFTED OFF THE BOARD BY THE WINNING PLAYER.

The game ends when the king can't avoid capture. Checkmate is like taking the king hostage.

Why Was Chess Invented?

As long as kings have fought battles, they have needed cunning and foresight. Listen to old legends (like the *Iliad* or the ancient Indian epic *Mahabharata*) and you'll hear stories of how armies won and lost.

Soldiers train to increase their strength and their skill with weapons. Kings and generals need to develop their mental agility. They must use their troops swiftly and well.

Chess may have started as just such a training exercise. It was first played sometime before 600 AD in northern India.

(continued on next page)

MEET THE FIGHTERS
. . . PAWNS AND PIECES

(continued from previous page)

That game had a vizier — a high court official — instead of the queen. The bishops were elephants, the knights were just horses, and the rooks were chariots.

When the game spread to Western Europe in the Middle Ages, chessmen assumed their current names and shapes.

Kings and generals, kids and grownups still play chess — even computers now play chess. Good players keep an eye on their opponent's chessmen as well as on their own.

THE LITTLE GUYS . . . THE PAWNS

Each player has eight pawns. If you think of chess as a battle, then these are the infantry, the foot soldiers who bear the brunt of an attack. They fill the front row, acting as the first line of defense.

Like ordinary soldiers, pawns can be promoted on the battlefield after they've broken through enemy lines and reached the opponent's back row. So, even though they may start out as the least valuable chessmen, they can end up as powerful as the queen!

THE OFFICER CLASS . . . THE PIECES

Players also have eight more chessmen known collectively as "the pieces." They all go on the back row. There are two rooks, two knights, and two bishops, but only one king and one queen.

ROOKS LIKE A CASTLE TO ME

Rook is the odd, but traditional, name of the castle-shaped chessmen at either end of the back row. Rooks get more useful later in the game when there are fewer chessmen left on the board to get in their way.

KNIGHTS ON HORSEBACK

Knights look like horses and jump like them, too. Athletic and unpredictable, knights leap over friend and enemy alike.

BISHOPS AND THEIR HATS

Bishops have the slit hat called a mitre. They start the game on either side of the king and queen, recalling the time when the great lords of the church helped kings to rule.

THE MIGHTY QUEEN

The queen is smaller than the king, and wears a simpler crown, but don't be taken in — she's the most dangerous piece there is. The queen's job is to protect her own king and lead the fight to capture her opponent's king.

THE KING (MORE OF A WORRY THAN YOU'D EXPECT)

All the other chessman can be captured without ending the game. When the king is cornered, he is "in check." When the king is caught, the game is over — it's "checkmate." He does have a little power, but the king's real importance is as a target, to protect or capture.

THE CHECKERED BOARD

Chess is always played on a board with 64 squares. Neither the board nor the chessmen have to be black and white. The light-colored pieces and squares are usually called white, and the dark ones are called black. This makes identifying the opposing sides easier.

NO CROWDING!

Only one chessman may stand on any square at a time. When a chessman captures another, the captured piece is taken off the board.

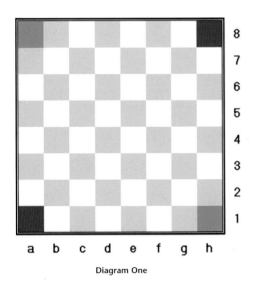

Diagram One

WHITE ON THE RIGHT

Each time you set up the board, both players should have a white square in the right-hand corner of their back row, and a black square in the left-hand corner. Players rhyme white with right to remind themselves of this. (Diagram One)

SETTING UP THE CHESSMEN

THE BACK ROW

Black players should set their pieces up from left to right on their back row in this order: (Diagram Two)

Rook, Knight, Bishop, King, Queen, Bishop, Knight, Rook

White players should set up their pieces, the chessmen, from left to right on their back row in this order: (Diagram Two)

Rook, Knight, Bishop, Queen, King, Bishop, Knight, Rook

THE FRONT ROW

The eight pawns go directly in front, on the second row.
Some tips to help you here:

THE QUEEN STICKS TO HER COLORS

- When setting up the chessmen, always put the queen on a square that matches her color. The White queen goes on a white square; the Black queen goes on a black square.

EYE TO EYE: THE KINGS SQUARE OFF

- The kings are the tallest pieces, and they always face each other across the board.

WHITE STARTS

- The White player makes the first move. The Black move, that which follows, is called the "reply." Players alternate moves throughout the game. If you play several games in a row, you should change sides after each game so each player gets a chance to start the action.

Diagram Two
The Starting Position

HOW BISHOPS MOVE, ATTACK, AND ARE OBSTRUCTED

MOVE

Bishops move diagonally, always staying on the same color square. (Diagram Three)

Bishops can never be blocked by the other bishop on their own side.

The longest move a bishop can make is seven squares, from one corner of the board to the other. In real games their moves are almost always much shorter.

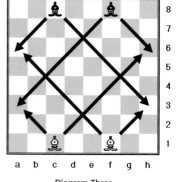

Diagram Three
The Bishop's Moves

Bishops are most useful in the center of the board, where they can dart forward or backward as needed.

ATTACK

A bishop attacks by moving straight to the square of an enemy piece and capturing it. He has no special attacking movement.

OBSTRUCTED

A bishop can be blocked by a chessman from his own side, since he cannot jump over it.

Diagram Four

Here is a little practice just to try. You have nine moves and nine pieces to take with your black bishop. How do you do it? Think carefully.

Diagram Four

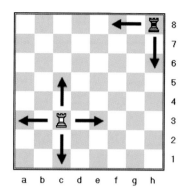

Diagram Five
The Rook's Moves

HOW ROOKS MOVE, ATTACK, AND ARE OBSTRUCTED

MOVE

Rooks plod in a straight line forward, backward, or sideways — but never diagonally. (Diagram Five)

ATTACK

A rook attacks by knocking out any enemy chessman in its path. The captured chessman is taken off the board, and the rook occupies its square instead. Like the bishop, the rook attacks in the same way he normally moves.

OBSTRUCTED

Any chessman from the rook's own side stops it in its tracks. Rooks cannot jump over any piece.

Rooks are most useful either when twinned with the king in a special move discussed later called "castling," or toward the end of the game, when the board empties and the rooks can make long, swooping attacks.

Rookies

Rookies, or "learner" players, are named after rooks. Rookies are usually the last to be used in a game, just like the rooks in chess, which are usually deployed late.

Diagram Eight

Can you get the knight down to h1 in five moves? Can you get the knight over to a1 in six moves?

"Oh, what fun it is! How I *wish* I was one of them! I wouldn't mind being a pawn, if only I might join — though of course I should *like* to be a Queen best."

—*Alice Through the Looking Glass* by Lewis Carroll

HOW KNIGHTS MOVE, ATTACK, AND ARE OBSTRUCTED

MOVE

A knight looks like a horse and acts like one, too. It can jump over any chessmen in its path. Knights make an L-shaped move, going two squares forward or to the side, and then one square in the other direction. (Diagram Six)

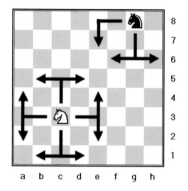

Diagram Six
The Knight's Moves

ATTACK

A knight attacks by leaping on an enemy chessman and taking its place. Knights don't take the chessmen they jump over, only those on whom they land.

OBSTRUCTED

A knight can be blocked if a chessman from his own side is already on the square on which he wants to land. Knights cannot land on their own pieces, but they can jump over them.

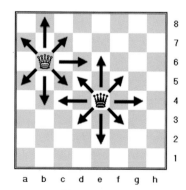

Diagram Seven
The Queen's Moves

HOW THE QUEEN MOVES, ATTACKS, AND IS OBSTRUCTED

MOVE

The queen moves like a rook, going forward, backward, and sideways. She also moves like a bishop, traveling on the diagonal. However, the queen cannot jump like a knight. (Diagram Seven)

ATTACK

When the queen attacks, she moves straight onto the enemy's square and occupies it herself.

OBSTRUCTED

If her own men get in the way, the queen is blocked and cannot move past them.

Queen Care

The queen is your most powerful piece, so use her wisely! Look before you move her. You don't want to have your queen taken because of your carelessness.

CHESSMEN IN ACTION   19

Good Manners That Keep You Out of Trouble

In competitions and other formal play, when you touch one of your chessmen, you have to move it. While you're learning or playing with friends, you don't have to stick to the "touch-move" rule. All the same, it's a good idea to get in the habit of only touching your chessmen when you want to move them. Should you notice that a chessman is not in the middle of its square, tell the other player before you adjust it, "I'm not taking my turn yet, I'm putting this piece back where it belongs."

HOW LITTLE THE KING CAN DO

MOVE

The king travels only one square per move, in any direction — forward or backward, diagonally or sideways. (Diagram Nine)

ATTACK

He can take all but one chessman. He can't attack the enemy king. Any other chessman who comes close enough is fair game.

Diagram Nine
The King's Moves

THE "KINGS APART" RULE

Warring kings must always keep one square between them. That middle square can be empty or occupied, but the gap is essential. In real games this means that one king can't capture the other unaided.

THE "IN CHECK" RULE

There is a special restriction on the king's freedom of movement. He's not allowed to put himself "in check" — that is, to put himself knowingly in the path of an enemy piece. That's why one king can't land on a square next to the other king.

You may think, "So what?" Nobody in their right mind would put the king in that kind of risk when losing the king means losing the game, would they? Actually, there are times when this would be sneakily useful — but you can't do it — rats!

King's X

Chess historians have many explanations for the ban on kings taking each other. Some say that it dates from the Golden Age of Chivalry. In those days, kings ruled by Divine Right, which means they believed God authorized them to reign. Killing an enemy king was an offense against God, so it could cost you your own right to the throne.

WHAT OTHERS DO TO THE KING

HOW THE KING IS OBSTRUCTED, ATTACKED, CHECKED, AND CHECKMATED

CHECKED: Checked is when your opponent makes a move that directly threatens the king. If the king doesn't use his next move to get himself out of trouble, he will be captured, or checkmated.

CHECKMATED: Checkmate ends the game. That is when the opponent makes a move that leaves the king with no way to get to safety.

OBSTRUCTED: The king cannot jump, so he can be blocked by his own side. As he is usually being sheltered from trouble, this tends to be more protection than problem.

ATTACKED: The king is the most vulnerable piece because if you lose him you lose the game. He spends most of his time surrounded by his own side. When one of his protection squad is taken out of play, that may count as "check," since it could lead to his being taken.

QUIZ NO. 1
- Who can check the king? (Diagram Ten)

Answer upside down page 23.

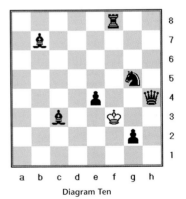

Diagram Ten

LEARN CHESS FAST

HOW PAWNS MOVE, ATTACK, ARE OBSTRUCTED, AND IGNORE EACH OTHER

Diagram Eleven

FIRST MOVE

The first time any pawn moves, it may advance straight ahead two squares instead of the usual one. The purpose of this rule is to speed up the game's early stage. It also loosens up the front rows to let the pieces in the back row out sooner. (Diagram Eleven)

THE MOVES THAT FOLLOW

After that first step, pawns move a single square at a time. They can't reverse — they only go forward.

ATTACK

Pawns have another important trick up their sleeves: they can only capture by moving diagonally. An attacking pawn moves one diagonal square forward. At all other times, they only move straight ahead. (Diagram Twelve)

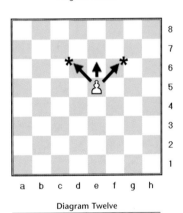

Diagram Twelve

*A Pawn's diagonal move is a capture move.

*Answer to Quiz No. 1: The pawn on e4 can, but the pawn on g2 can't, since pawns can't go backward. The bishop on b7 could if the pawn on e4 moved, but the bishop on c3 never will, since it's a bishop who only travels on black squares and the White king is on a white one. The knight on g5 can, as can the rook on f8. The queen on h4 would need two moves to do it, since there is no straight path from the White king to the Black queen.

OBSTRUCTED

It's important to remember that an enemy piece in the square immediately in front of a pawn blocks it. When pawns go nose to nose with enemy pawns, they just get stuck.

After a pawn has attacked on the diagonal, it finds itself in the "file," or row of squares, next to its original path. The pawn then goes straight ahead in that new "file." (Diagram Thirteen, Diagram Fourteen)

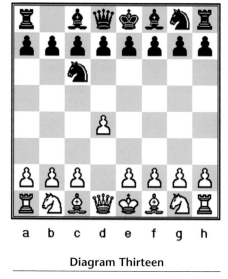

Diagram Thirteen

The White pawn took his first move forward two spaces. Black's opening move was to jump his knight forward. Do you see that if the White pawn doesn't move (or protect it) next turn, the Black knight could capture it?

PAWN PROMOTED!

When a pawn makes the long journey down to the opponent's back rank (1 for a Black pawn, 8 for a White), the pawn can turn into any other more powerful piece, except the king.

The best bet is probably to make the pawn a queen, although you could choose a rook, knight, or bishop.

- If you've lost your queen, replace the pawn with the queen and she's back in play.
- If your queen is still in the game, but one of your rooks is not, turn it upside down and use it as a second queen.
- If you still have your rooks and your queen, lay the pawn on its side to show that it has been promoted to a queen.

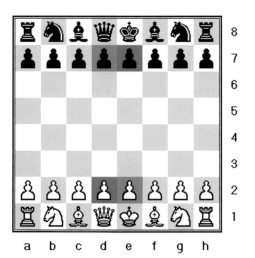

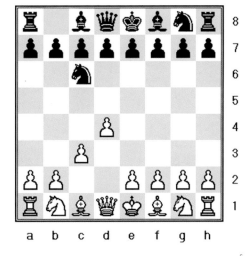

Diagram Fourteen

White can protect the pawn on square d4 by bringing another pawn forward. This time the pawn only moves one step, though, to square c3. You see, if the Black knight does take the pawn on d4, then the other pawn can use the diagonal capturing move to take it. Now the two pawns protect each other. If the Black knight takes the White pawn, he'll be taken himself. That looks like a bad deal to Black, so the pawns are safe.

Diagram Fifteen
Not All Pawns Are Created Equal

Even though your pawns look the same, the pawns in the middle rows of the board are more active because they control the important central territory. Moving the middle pawns quickly un-blocks the queen and bishops in the back row behind them.

MESSAGES FROM THE BATTLEFIELD

READING THE BOARD: CHESS NOTATION

When chess players want to discuss what happened once play has ended, they need a way of describing and remembering the action. They make a diagram of the game.

Chess diagrams aren't hard to figure out. It's worth the effort, even for beginners. You can follow other people's games and remember your own.

Put a board in front of you as you read this, so you can check out each part for yourself.

Remember, "White rhymes with right," so the right-hand corner nearest you should be white. (That way the board is correctly situated.)

The White queen sits on her white square to start, so the White chessmen are always shown as if they were closest to you. In a diagram, they are at the bottom of the board.

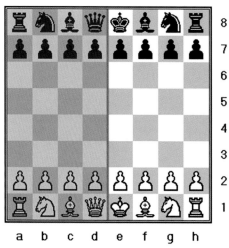

Diagram Sixteen

KING'S SIDE, QUEEN'S SIDE

The chessboard is divided into two equal parts. If you run a line down the middle of the board starting between your own king and queen, you will see that the Black and White queens are on the left and the two kings are on the right.

The left side is called the queen's side (see shaded side). The right side is called the king's side. (Diagram Sixteen)

NUMBERED RANK AND LETTERED FILE

You need to know how to identify each square on the board.

For example, if you and a friend each have a chess set in your own house, you can play chess by phone or fax or e-mail. You each set up the game, and you each do the moves your opponent describes for you on your own board, just as he does for you. That way you both see the same game. But you need to agree how to identify the squares to be able to tell each other which moves to make.

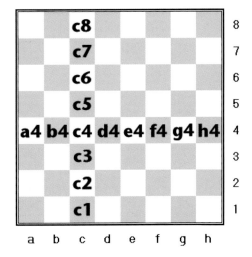

Diagram Seventeen

Squares running across the board from left to right are lettered from **a** to **h** — the first eight letters of the alphabet.

Thus the White queen always starts on **d** and White king always starts on **e**.

The squares running up the side of the board are numbered from the bottom to the top — from nearest you to farthest away — from **1** to **8**.

The White queen starts the game at **d1**. The Black queen starts at **d8**. The White pawns start in row **2** and the Black pawns start in row **7**. (Diagram Seventeen)

SHOWING THE ACTION

You need to show where a chessman starts and the moves he makes. That means you must have a way of showing the action.

The set of squares running from any lettered square to its twin across the board is called a "file."

The set of squares running between from any numbered square to its twin across the board is called a "rank."

Ranks span sideways across the board. Files go from bottom to top of the board. (Diagram Eighteen)

There are eight ranks and eight files, and each is eight squares long.

Try seeing which piece on this diagram is at **b2**, at **e6**, at **g1**, and at **f7**? (Diagram Nineteen)

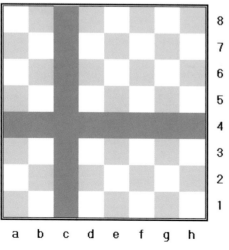

Diagram Eighteen

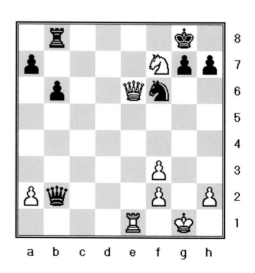

Diagram Nineteen

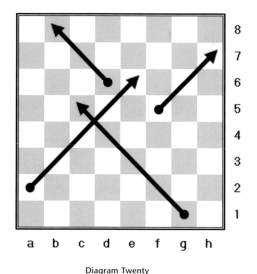

Diagram Twenty

QUIZ NO. 2

- Can you name these diagonals? (Diagram Twenty)

Answer upside down this page.

Funny Punctuation

...+!?x!!?? 0-0 0-0-0...+!?x !!?? 0-0 0-0-0...+!?x!!??0-0 0-0-0...+!?x !!??0-0 0-0-0

... means Black's move (1 ...e5)

+ means check

! means good move

!! means great move

? means bad move

?? means truly terrible move

x means capture

0-0 means king's side castling

0-0-0 means queen's side castling

DIAGONALS — THE LONG AND THE SHORT OF IT

Diagonals are the rows running from corner to corner. Diagonals are either all black or all white. The longest diagonals have eight squares and the shortest have two. These are the paths that bishops, queens and kings can take, and along which pawns can attack.

Chess notation doesn't have special names for diagonals as there are for rank and file rows. You describe a diagonal by naming the starting square and the ending square. Thus, a diagonal might be "**a2** to **g8**" or "**f1** to **h3**," or "**c8** to **h3**." (Diagram Twenty).

THE OPENING MOVES

The start of a chess game is called *the opening.*

Most players use the middle six pawns, and their bishops and knights, first. (Diagram Twenty-one)

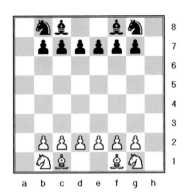

They tend to keep the queen out of action — and therefore danger — until the tight opening format has loosened up and more pieces are in the middle.

Side pawns and rooks may also stay behind to protect the king.

Players often start capturing enemy pieces only when they have their own chessmen fanned out towards the middle of the board.

That said, these are rules of thumb, not actual laws of play. You can also win by ignoring them, too! Good luck!

CAPTURE AND TRADE

CAPTURED PIECES

You may only get to capture an enemy chessman by sacrificing one of your own.

Maybe your own piece gets taken in your opponent's next turn.

Maybe, by deciding to hunt down the enemy, you left another piece exposed to danger.

The Action's Hottest in the Middle

Most play happens in the middle of the board, since that is where your "active" chessmen are closest to the opposing side. Don't forget to watch the whole board, though. Many a game has been won by sneaking in from the edges.

*Answer to Quiz No. 3: Black rook takes d8; h8; h7; h6; h3; b3; b6; and b7.

When you know your piece will be taken as a result of your capture, you have made a **trade**.

Knowing that capture rarely comes without cost, expert players have evolved an informal valuation of each piece.

This helps them decide when a capture is worth the risk, and when it isn't.

This is not scoring. Chess is a game in which you win or you lose. There is no scoring in a single game. It's all or nothing.

The only score you ever get in chess is when you count up the total number of games won in a formal match.

The least valuable chessman is the pawn — you have lots of them, and in comparison to a rook, knight, or bishop, they can't do much.

The most valuable chessman is the queen. You only have one of her, and she's dangerous.

Scoring is counted in points, with each point being worth one pawn. So...

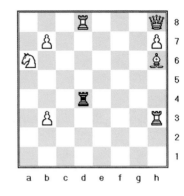

Diagram Twenty-two

VALUATION OF PIECES

1 queen = 9 points = 9 pawns
1 rook = 5 points = 5 pawns
1 knight = 3 points = 3 pawns
1 bishop = 3 points = 3 pawns

QUIZ NO. 3

• It is your move as black. Can you capture all eight pieces in exactly eight moves? Can you see two ways to do this?

Answer upside down page 32.

"That's chess," snapped Ron. "You've got to make some sacrifices! I take one step forward and she'll take me — that leaves you free to checkmate the king, Harry."

Harry Potter and the Sorcerer's Stone by J. K. Rowling

WINNING AND LOSING

PUTTING YOUR OPPONENT INTO CHECK

When you attack your opponent's king, you put him into "check."

You have checked your opponent when your next move will capture the king.

If the king can't escape, then the check is actually checkmate.

It's polite to say "check" when you make this sort of move. It alerts your opponent to the danger.

Whoever is in check must get out of check in the next move or lose the game.

When you see a "+" sign in chess notation, it comes at the end of a move that "checks" the opponent.

GET ME OUT OF CHECK!

The worst has almost happened — you're in check! What can you do? Your solution will be one of the following:

MOVE THE KING

- Can you move the king out of harm's way? Start by looking for an adjacent square where he isn't threatened.

CAPTURE THE CHECKING PIECE

- Can you beat the threat by taking out the checking piece yourself? Look to see who's around to help you.

> "'Now then,' said her father good-humouredly, 'don't forget who taught you chess. I remember a time when you thought a fool's mate was the most brilliant chess sequence invented.'"
>
> — *millennium @drumshee* by Cora Harrison

Diagram Twenty-three

Diagram Twenty-four

BLOCK, BLOCK, BLOCK!

Might you obstruct the checking piece by moving something into its path? This won't work against an attacking knight who jumps over anything in his way.

Here are some examples of check.

- Diagram Twenty-three: This is check. White can escape by moving his king to **g2** or **h2**.
- Diagram Twenty-four: This is more serious. White is in check from the Black rook, since White's pawns have trapped their own king. White has no escape route, so this is checkmate, not check.

QUIZ NO. 4:
Here's the kind of situation you might meet. White's king is in check from Black's queen on **b4**. (Diagram Twenty-five)

The three ways of stopping the check are:
- White can move the king to **f1**, to **e2**, or to **d1**.(Diagram Twenty-six)
- White can take the Black queen with **Qb7xb4**. (Note that the chessmen themselves are represented by a capital letter.) (Diagram Twenty-seven)
- White can block the check. White could use **c2-c3**, **Nb1-c3**, **Nb1-d2**, or **Bc1-d2**. ("N" stands for "knight.") (Diagram Twenty-eight)
Which do you think is the Smart Move?*

Answer upside down this page

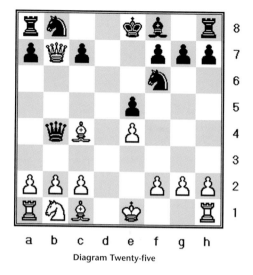

Diagram Twenty-five

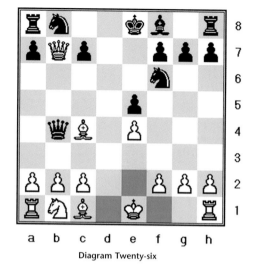

Diagram Twenty-six

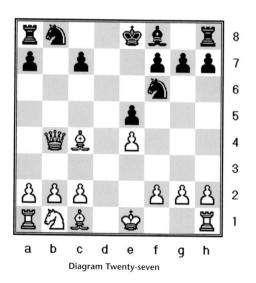

Diagram Twenty-seven

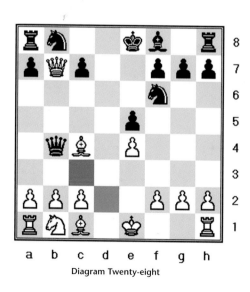

Diagram Twenty-eight

AS THE SAYING GOES, "YOU CAN FOOL SOME OF THE PEOPLE SOME OF THE TIME . . ."

HOW TO WIN IN TWO MOVES (WITH LUCK AND AGAINST A COMPLETE BEGINNER)

This is so simple, you can probably only do it once to the same person, even when playing a younger brother or sister.

Unfortunately, you can only do it if your opponent makes the moves that set the stage for your attack.

Your opponent may not make those moves in the first few moves. Keep an eye out, though — you may sometimes be able to play this set of moves later in the game.

Your opponent is White, you are Black.

Diagram Twenty-nine: 1. **g2-g4** White's first move — As always, white makes the first move. White moves the pawn in front of the knight closest to White's king forward two spaces. This begins to unblock a diagonal line straight to the king.

Diagram Thirty: 1. **e7-e5** (or **e6**) Black's first move — Black moves the pawn in front of the king forward two spaces as well. This move frees the Black queen.

Diagram Thirty-one: 2. **f2-f4** (or **f3**) White's second move — White moves the pawn in front of his white-square bishop forward. Do you see the danger approaching?

Diagram Thirty-two: 2. **Qd8-h4** checkmate. Black queen scoots straight to the edge of the board at **h4**. From there, in her next move, she can attack the White king.

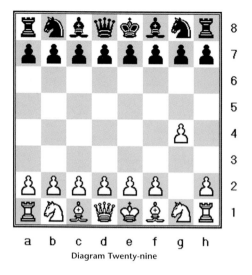

Diagram Twenty-nine

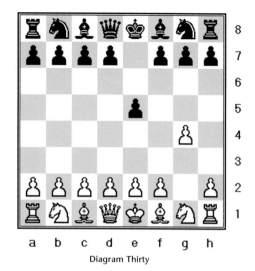

Diagram Thirty

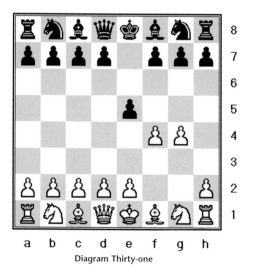

Diagram Thirty-one

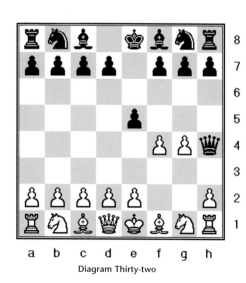

Diagram Thirty-two

The White king is hemmed in. The only move he can make is to **f2**, right in the path of the Black queen. When there is no escape, the result is checkmate.

FOOL'S MATE WORKS ONLY IF . . .

- Your opponent's king is hemmed in like this. (Diagram Thirty-three)
- Your opponent pulls the pawn on file **f** at least one square forward and the pawn on file **g** two squares forward. (Diagram Thirty-four)
- You can get your queen to **h4**. (Diagram Thirty-five)

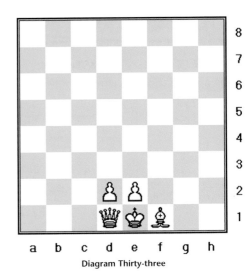

Diagram Thirty-three

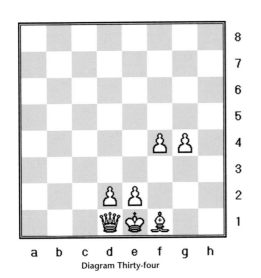

Diagram Thirty-four

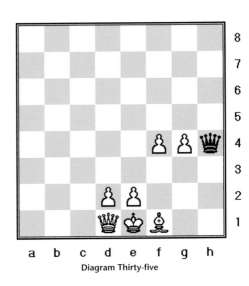

Diagram Thirty-five

THE CASTLED KING OR QUEEN

KING'S OR QUEEN'S SIDE CASTLING

This is a special move that allows the king to act as a team with one of his rooks. It is a good move because it is the only time that the king can travel more than one square at a time. He also ends up farther from threats, tucked away on **g1** or **c1**.

NEITHER THE KING NOR THE ROOK MAY HAVE MOVED BEFORE. IT MUST BE THEIR FIRST MOVE.KING'S SIDE CASTLING: "0-0"

ARRGH! YIKES! HURRAH! CHECKMATE!

CHECKMATE ENDS THE GAME.

Sometimes you see that checkmate is coming several moves before it actually happens.

Experienced players often "resign" at this point. They know they've lost, and they avoid the last few depressing moves.

All the same, DON'T EVER RESIGN!!!! Why?
• Because your opponent may not see the checkmate.
• Because your opponent might goof up.

Tough it out to the end — it's good practice.

Get the knight and bishop out of the way, leaving the squares between the king and rook empty.

The action starts when the player says, "I'm castling," to alert his opponent.

King's side castling looks like this: Diagram Thirty-six (before), Diagram Thirty-seven (after).

The rook has leapt over the king. How this rule got onto the books is one of the mysteries of chess.

QUEEN'S SIDE CASTLING: "0-0-0"

Queen's side castling is harder than king's side castling because you have the extra work of shifting the queen off the back row before you move. (Diagram Thirty-eight)

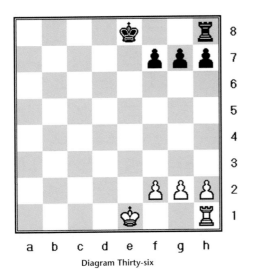

Diagram Thirty-six

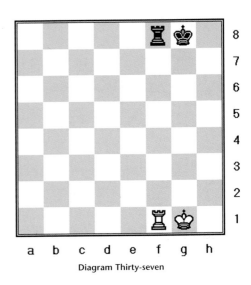

Diagram Thirty-seven

CHECK STOPS CASTLING

Something more to remember:

- The king can't castle if he is in check when he starts the move or if he will be when he finishes. Castling is not a way of rescuing a king in danger. That means the king can't cross any square where, if he were to stay, he'd be in check.

Watch out for threats on **f1** and **g1** for king's side castling, and on **d1** and **c1** for queen's side castling. A threat to those vacant squares counts as a threat to the king.

Why can't Black castle here? (Diagram Thirty-nine) Answer below.

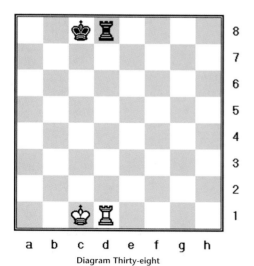

Diagram Thirty-eight

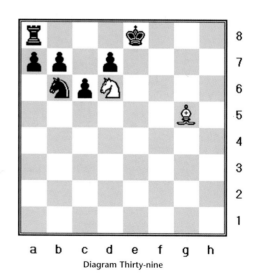

Diagram Thirty-nine

*Answer: Black cannot castle because the black king is in check and the white bishop controls square d8 — either would be enough to prevent castling.

SCHOLAR'S MATE

OR HOW TO WIN YOUR SCHOOL TOURNAMENT

SCHOLAR'S MATE HAS TWO CRUCIAL LESSONS TO TEACH:

- Always try to figure out the threat behind an opponent's move.
- Try to prevent your opponent from pressuring a weak square in your own position. In this game, Black's weak square is **f7**. Watch it throughout the game.

Like most chess combinations, it is easy to escape if you see it coming — and hard to avoid if you don't!

Play this out as you read. You are White (though you could just as easily be Black).

Diagram Forty: 1. **e2-e4** White starts by bringing out the **e** pawn two spaces. This move is a standard one because it's very practical. The White queen is already free to move, as is the white-square bishop.

Diagram Forty-one: 1. ...**e7-e5** Black answers with the same move. Black's queen and black-square bishop are also ready to roll.

Diagram Forty-two: 2. **Bf1-c4** White king's bishop, the one who travels on white squares, is sent forward. He stops on an important square, **c4**. Whom can he attack from there? (Answer below)

Diagram Forty-three: 2. ...**Bf8-c5** Black copies White's move once more.

Scholar's Mate exploits the power of the diagonal in chess. White uses diagonal moves on the white squares to threaten and then to checkmate Black.

Answer: The black pawn on **f7** is under attack.

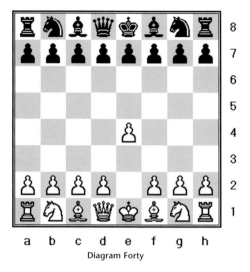

Diagram Forty

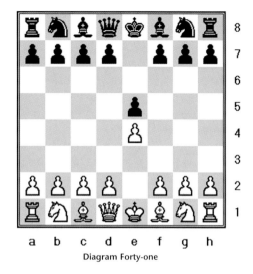

Diagram Forty-one

Diagram Forty-two

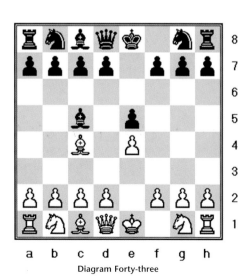

Diagram Forty-three

Diagram Forty-four

Diagram Forty-five: 3. **Qd1-h5** White's queen arrives on **h5**. She poses a particular threat to the Black pawn on **f7**.

- Both she and the White bishop can take this pawn.
- The **f7** pawn's only protection is the king. The undefended Black pawn on **e5** is also at risk.

Another way to attack **f7** is by moving 3. **Qf3**.

Diagram Forty-six: 3. ...**Nb8-c6** Black goofs. Black protects the pawn on **e5**, but he misses the bigger threat. Can you see it?

Diagram Forty-seven: 4. **Qh5-xf7** checkmate. White's queen captures the pawn on **f7**. This is checkmate because the king cannot save himself.

- If the Black king takes the White queen on **f7**, then the White bishop on **c4** takes him.
- If the Black king moves to the empty **e7** or **f8** squares, the White queen takes him.
- If the Black king stays put, the White queen takes him.

Diagram Forty-eight: What would have saved Black? ...**Qd8-e7** would have protected the **e5** pawn and stopped the pending checkmate dead.

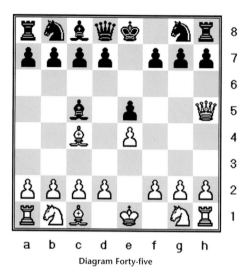

Diagram Forty-five

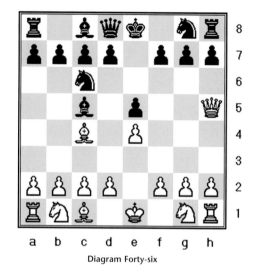

Diagram Forty-six

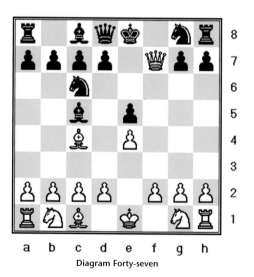

Diagram Forty-seven

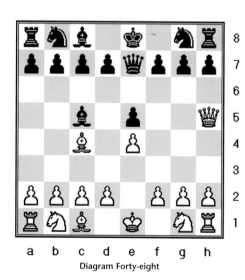

Diagram Forty-eight

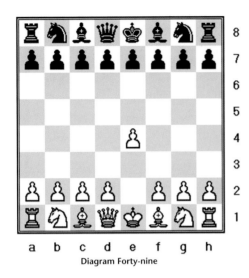

Diagram Forty-nine

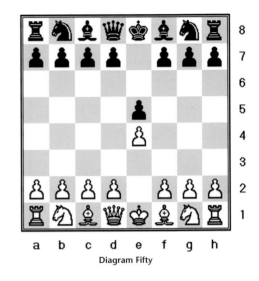

Diagram Fifty

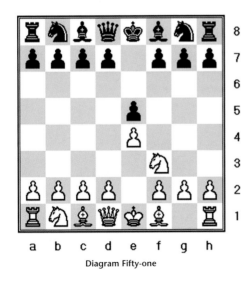

Diagram Fifty-one

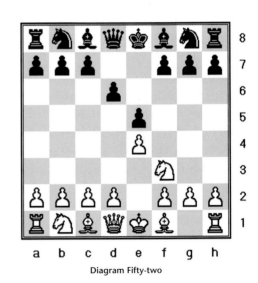

Diagram Fifty-two

Legall's Mate

Practice this game. Decide where your opponent could block you.

To be effective, you need to be ready to abandon Legall's Mate, and then to return to it if the board changes.

FOR REAL EXPERTS . . . LEGALL'S MATE

Legall's Mate helps you beat those kids who know only Scholar's Mate. It's worth practicing if you're facing an opponent who's probably as good as you are — so you've got a trick up your sleeve.

Monsieur de Kermur (whose title was the Sire de Legall) was chess champion of France 250 years ago. He specialized in "combination play," which means he would use a move for the purpose of hiding a secondary threat. This is the game he's most remembered for.

Diagram Forty-nine: 1. **e2-e4** This is a standard, sensible opening that gives little away.

Diagram Fifty: 1. ... **e7-e5** An equally sensible response, which could lead anywhere.

Now both sides can get their queens and a bishop out onto the open board.

Diagram Fifty-one: 2. **Ng1-f3** White starts to move the knights out. Their location will be crucial for the later "pin" that locks the Black king into checkmate.

Diagram Fifty-two: 2. ... **d7-d6** Black concentrates on bringing his pawns forward. Ask yourself what is now free to come forward?

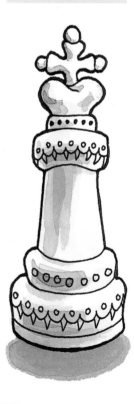

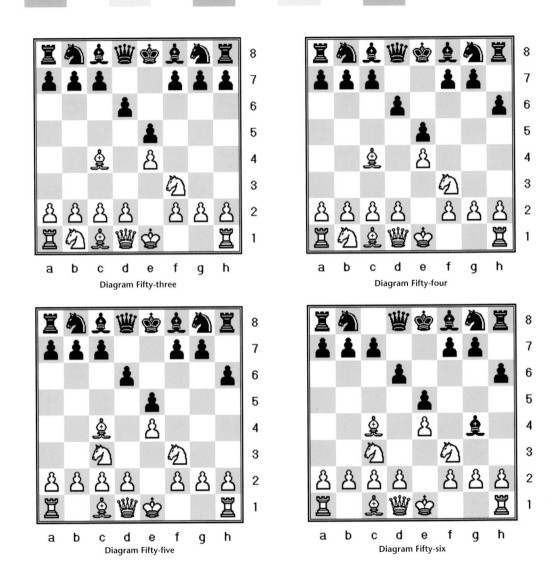

Diagram Fifty-three

Diagram Fifty-four

Diagram Fifty-five

Diagram Fifty-six

Diagram Fifty-three: 3. **Bf1-c4** White's bishop starts the journey that leads to a kill. Why stop on **c4**?

Diagram Fifty-four: 3. ...**h7-h6** What speedy getaway is helped by bringing a flanking pawn forward?

Diagram Fifty-five: 4. **Nb1-c3** Out comes the other knight.

Diagram Fifty-six: 4. ...**Bc8-g4** Now that Black matches White's last move, look to the line of pawns. What might happen back there now? Does Black help White by opening his rear file up, or does he set the stage for some fast action of his own?

> "He clenched his teeth and stared in disbelief as piece after piece fell to Baraka; and he saw clearly that in one move more the cat would checkmate him."
>
> — *The Town Cats and Other Tales* by Lloyd Alexander (1977, reissued 2000)

ONE OF THE TWO SHORTEST GAMES EVER PLAYED IN A TOURNAMENT:
DJORDJEVIC - KOVACEVIC, BELA CRKVA 1984

1. d4 Nf6 (Diagram Fifty-seven)

2. Bg5 c6 (Diagram Fifty-eight)

3. e3 Qa5+ (Diagram Fifty-nine)

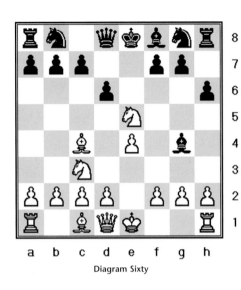

Diagram Sixty

Diagram Sixty: 5. **Nf3xe5** White's knight takes a pawn. Would it have been worth taking if better defended? Who could have defended it?

You'll see that White needs both knights for his trick to work. What fourth move by Black would have stopped White from being able to make this move?

See how you can dangle a prize in front of your opponent to keep him from noticing your devious plans!

Diagram Sixty-one: 5. **...Bg4xd1** A coup for Black — or was it tempting bait, left available to keep Black's eye down the board where he thinks he can win? At first sight it is a good trade for Black — a bishop for a queen.

Diagram Sixty-two: 6. **Bc4xf7+** White checks the Black king. But it doesn't look that dangerous . . . Or does it?

Diagram Sixty-three: 6. **...Ke8-e7** The Black king slides out of trouble . . . he thinks! Is there a better move Black could have made?

Diagram Sixty-four: 7. **Nc3-d5** checkmate Now the true cleverness of this three-pronged attack is revealed. If the Black king moves to **e8** or **e6**, he is taken by the White bishop. If he tries **d7**, the White knight on **e5** takes him. If he stays put, the White knight on **d5** performs the capture. Black loses.

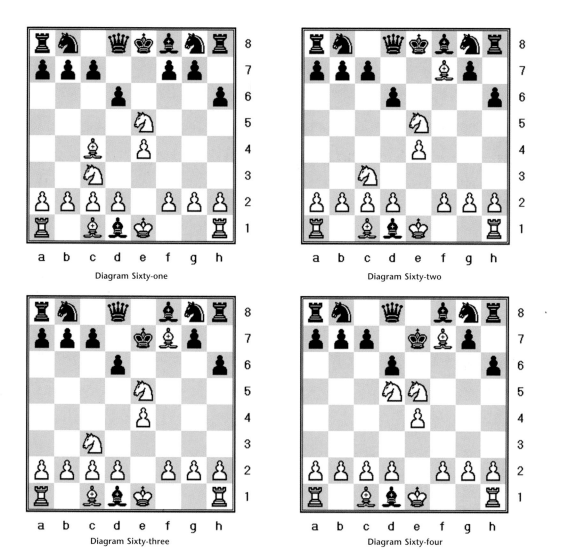

Diagram Sixty-one

Diagram Sixty-two

Diagram Sixty-three

Diagram Sixty-four

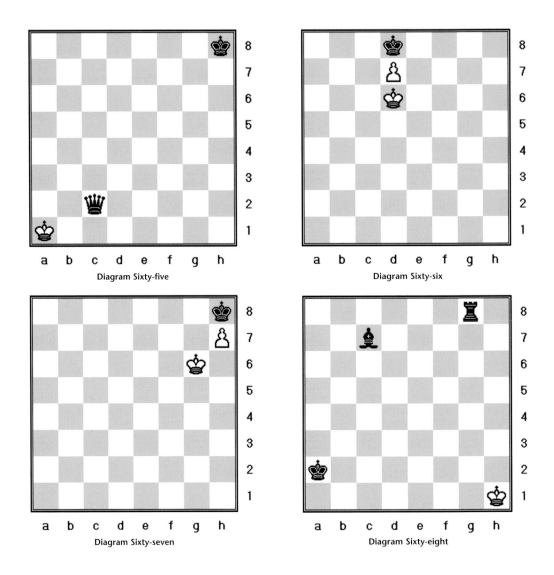

Diagram Sixty-five

Diagram Sixty-six

Diagram Sixty-seven

Diagram Sixty-eight

STALEMATE

WHAT IS STALEMATE?

White is to move, and it is stalemate. White has no legal move, so the game is automatically a draw. (Diagram Sixty-five)

Black is to move, and it is stalemate. (Diagram Sixty-six)

Black is to move, and it is stalemate. (Diagram Sixty-seven)

Stalemate is when neither side can win. If you absolutely cannot win a game, you may try to set a trap that leads to stalemate, even if you have lost your queen. One king can never take another, so their direct confrontation is a draw, which is better than a loss.

White is to move, and the result is stalemate again. (Diagram Sixty-eight)

HOW DO YOU GUARD AGAINST STALEMATE?

When you are ahead by a comfortable margin, it is tempting to take away square after square from the enemy king and plan to checkmate later. This can lead to stalemate, so it is a good idea to try to give check with each move of the end game. This avoids the danger of stalemate.

Oddly, "king and rook *versus* king" and "king and queen *versus* king" are easy wins, but not ones where you can check often on your way to checkmate. There is a greater risk of stalemate with these end games.

"How can I lose to such an idiot?" wailed Chess genius Aron Nimzovich (1886-1935). Begs the question: Who's the "idiot?"

Deep Blue

IBM's Deep Blue was created by three post-graduate students at Pittsburgh's Carnegie-Mellon University in 1985. It can access and evaluate every possible move at a speed of 200 million positions per second. Garry Kasparov, fifteen-year World Champion until 2000, is among the fastest human chess thinkers. He can only evaluate three chess positions per second.

STALEMATE CAN RESULT FROM BEING TOO CAUTIOUS.

Black decides he is going to corner the White king so there is no way for the king to get out of the trap in the following move. When Black plays **...Rh8** the result is stalemate. (Diagram Sixty-nine)

The right way out of this problem would be:

1. **...Rg7+**
2. **Kh2 Rh8** checkmate (Diagram Seventy)

When you have a "king and queen *versus* king," you can't checkmate with the queen by continually checking because the king keeps escaping.

Checking over and over with the queen is useless. Try it, and you won't be able to give checkmate this way against a strong defense. (Diagram Seventy-one)

Another wrong solution is to try to clamp the king down in your first move. The result is stalemate after **Qc7**.

The right solution is to play:

1. **Kc6 Kb8**
2. **Qb7 checkmate** (Diagram Seventy-two)

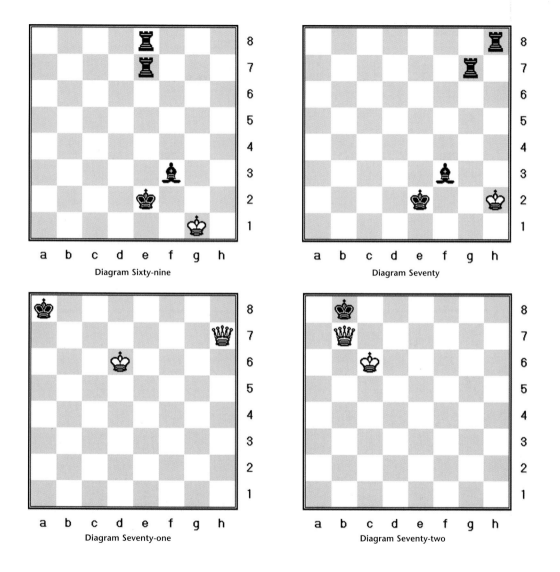

Diagram Sixty-nine

Diagram Seventy

Diagram Seventy-one

Diagram Seventy-two

The same problem happens with "king and rook *versus* king." If you keep checking with the rook here, you'll never get to checkmate. (Diagram Seventy-three)

There are two ways to win this without first giving check. Solution one is:

1. **Kg6 Kg8**
2. **Ra8 checkmate**
   (Diagram Seventy-four)

Solution two is:

1. **Kf7 Kh7**
2. **Rh1 checkmate**
   (Diagram Seventy-five)

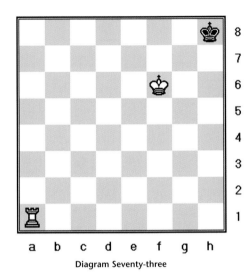

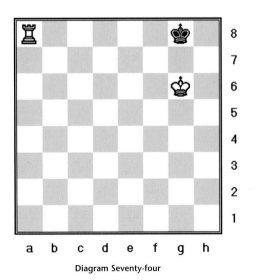

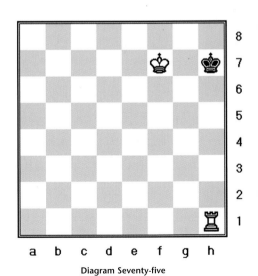

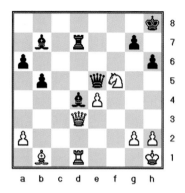

Diagram Seventy-six

COULD THIS HAVE BEEN THE STUPIDEST MOMENT IN CHESS HISTORY?

Von Popiel was White, Marco was Black. They played in an international tournament in Monaco in 1902. This is the board as Black starts his 36th move of the game. (Diagram Seventy-six)

Black resigned to avoid losing his bishop on **d4**. However, he could have won instantly by moving his bishop down to **g1**. Black now threatens the White queen as well as ...**Qxh2** mate!

The moral of this story: Always watch for your opponent to do something unexpectedly dumb. It's an easier way to win (if less rewarding) than by doing something smart yourself!

The Smallest Chess Set Ever Made

It fits on the flat, round head of an ordinary pin. This tiny set was first displayed at the Warsaw Museum of Technology in Poland in 1999. How do you think you could move the pieces?

61

A BIG MISTAKE

Brain and Brawn — Chess Whiz and Striker!

Norwegian Simen Agdestein was 16th in world chess rankings in 1989 and had also played eight matches for Norway's National Soccer team.

Age 15 in 1982: Simen was Chess Champion of Norway.

Age 18 in 1985: Simen was the Youngest Grandmaster in the entire world.

Age 21 in 1988: Simen made his soccer debut for Norway in a match against Italy as a striker.

FREQUENTLY ASKED QUESTIONS

CAN I MAKE A PAWN INTO AN EXTRA KING?

Never. You can have only one king per player.

CAN I MAKE A QUEEN WHEN I STILL HAVE ONE?

Yes. You can make all eight pawns into queens if you can get them promoted.

DO I HAVE TO CAPTURE?

Unlike checkers, you don't have to capture your opponent's chess-men. The only exception is when capturing offers your only legal move.

Here is an example of when White must capture (Diagram Seventy-seven):

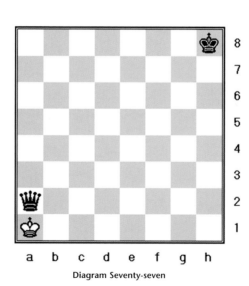

Diagram Seventy-seven

SHOULD I CAPTURE IF I CAN?

Yes! Not capturing often leads to losing a piece yourself. If you trade for a piece of equal value, do capture.

If you trade for a piece of greater value, do capture.

If you trade for a piece of lesser value, don't capture (don't trade your queen for a knight).

Don't worry about falling into a secret trap that is part of a cunning plan, as long as you can tell what your opponent intends to do. Chances are that you see more possibilities than your opponent does anyway.

CAN I HAVE TWO BISHOPS ON THE SAME COLOR SQUARES?

No, unless you promoted a pawn into a bishop. (Why would you when you could make it a queen?)

CAN I GIVE CHECKMATE WITH "BISHOP AND KING VERSUS KING?"

No, it is impossible. The king can always get away. The bishop and king together can't cover enough squares.

CAN I GIVE CHECKMATE WITH "KNIGHT AND KING VERSUS KING?"

No, it is impossible for the same reason as with bishop and king.

WHAT IF I GET TO "KING VERSUS KING?"

You have to stop play. Kings can't take each other, so you must agree to a draw.

CAN I GIVE CHECKMATE WITH "KING AND ROOK VERSUS KING?"

Yes, always. It is very easy. You do have to make sure to drive the opposing king to the back or side of the board.

CAN I GIVE CHECKMATE WITH "KING AND QUEEN VERSUS KING?"

Yes, it is even easier than with a rook. Just drive the king to the edge of the board.

DOES WHITE ALWAYS START FIRST?

Yes.

DO KNIGHTS ALWAYS END UP ON A DIFFERENT-COLORED SQUARE FROM THE ONE ON WHICH THEY STARTED?

Yes, always.

Disney heroines Belle, in *Beauty and the Beast*, and Mulan both play chess.

KEEP ON PLAYING!

You can play more chess now than at any time in history. You can play at home, at school, with friends, in competitions, on the internet, even in some parks and playgrounds.

SOME POINTERS FOR FUTURE GREATNESS (AND FUN ON THE WAY):

- The more you play, the better you'll get.

- Try to play at least some games against players who can beat you easily. You can improve faster that way. It's not the losing that helps — it's seeing how they won.

- Many kids and adults find that for them the most convenient chess battles are located on internet sites.

- The United States Chess Federation (USCF) offers a chess magazine, access to competitions, and internet play. Scholastic members must be fourteen or younger. They get a quarterly magazine, *School Mates*, and supervised internet play. Scholastic membership costs only US$13 per year (plus $2 if you live in Canada or Mexico, or plus $5 if you live elsewhere in the world).

STICK TO SAFE SITES LIKE:

- Contact the United States Chess Federation via their
  website (www.uschess.org)

  To join, call 800-388-5464, or write to:
  USCF Membership Department
  3054 US Rte. 9W
  New Windsor, NY 12553

- Contact the British Chess Federation via their website
  (www.bcf.ndirect.co.uk), or write to:
  The Watch Oak
  Chain Lane, Battle
  East Sussex, TN33 OYD

Castling: When king and rook act as one piece and move together.

Check: An attack on the king that he can avoid.

Checkmate: This is the winning move, when the king is in check and can't escape. It ends the game.

Diagonal: The lines of all Black or all White squares that slant across the board.

Draw: A chess game that ends without a winner. Neither player can beat the other, so the game is abandoned.

End Game: The final moves, which finish the chess game.

En Passant: A pawn can capture an opposing pawn (but not any other chessman) on its first move when it advances two squares instead one.

Exchange: To trade pieces.

File: The rows of squares that run up and down the board from your side to the opponent's side.

The Flank: The sides of the chess board, including the **a**, **b**, **g**, and **h** files.

Fork: Attacking two or more pieces at once.

King's Side: The halfside of the board from the kings' file to the edge of the board at the beginning of the game.

Mate: A less formal way of saying checkmate.

Pin: An attack against a piece that prevents it from moving.

Promotion: A name for the transformation a pawn achieves when he reaches the opposing side's back rank. Pawns are normally promoted to queen.

Queen's Side: The halfside of the board from the queens' file to the side of the board at the beginning of the game.

Rank: The rows of squares that cross the board from side to side.

Stalemate: Like a Draw, this is a game without a winner. It happens when the king can't move without placing himself in check.

> "Do you play?"
> ..."We all do," I told her. "My father really likes it. He says it's the best game in the world — good for the brain, helps you to think, he says. I can beat Rula and Mum every time. Never beaten Dad though."
> — *Black Queen* by Michael Morpurgo (Young Corgi 2000)

Bishop

Rook

Queen

Pawn

King

knight

QUICK REVIEW OF CHESSMEN AND HOW THEY MOVE

White moves first, then, alternates with Black. The chessmen are laid out the same on the chessboard. When you capture a chessman, you take its place on the board.

QUEEN

The most powerful piece is the queen. The queen moves in any direction as many squares as desired as long as her own pieces do not block her. She moves either forward, backward, sideways or on the diagonal. She captures anything in her path.

KING

The king is weak, but he is the most important piece, since without the king, you lose. Like the queen, he moves in any direction, but only one square per move. You win by surrounding your opponent's king, which is called checkmate. An attack on the king is called a check. It must always be countered immediately.

ROOKS

The second most powerful pieces are the rooks. They look like castles. Rooks move and capture in straight lines forward, backward, and sideways.

BISHOP

The bishops and knights are worth the same, a little less than a rook. The bishop moves like a rook, but only on the diagonal. Each player has one bishop who travels the white square diagonals and one who travels the black square diagonals.

KNIGHTS

Knights can jump over anything in their path. They take a long time to get from one side of the board to the other. Knights move one square forward or back and two squares sideways, or they move two squares forward or back and one square sideways.

PAWNS

Pawns are the least valuable pieces. They can never go backward. Pawns move straight forward but capture on the diagonal. On a pawn's first move it may advance two squares. After that pawns move only a single square at a time. When a pawn reaches the last row of squares, it is "promoted" and can become a queen (or any other piece but the king), even if you already have one on the board.